Get to the Greene Sales

By

Justin M. Greene Sr.

June 2020

In loving memory of Callie Mae Baskin.

Table of Contents

About the Author

I got my first taste of sales in third grade at the age of 8. My experience was not the most traditional form of sales, but I was tasked with selling yearbook ads. The person who sold the most ads was the winner and would get to be a part of the "Royal Court" in the annual Coronation. I hit the ground running, asking all my family members and parent's co-workers to support me. I ended up winning, and the reward was being crowned Duke of third grade. After that, I had the bug, and it never left. Any time there was a competition at school that involved selling something with a tangible award or recognition, I was on it. In seventh grade, I attempted to start my own business by selling bracelets to my classmates. This business endeavor was very short-lived when I realized that you must balance out the costs of products versus the selling price of the item. I attempted to run again for a place in the Coronation in eighth grade. With my involvement in many extracurricular activities, I didn't have the time to focus. In high school, I worked part-time jobs at various places, starting from my tenth-grade year. From Kroger to Chuck E. Cheese (Yes, I had to be the mouse!), I became comfortable working with the general public very early in life. I also played sports, which helped me gain the competitive nature necessary for any type of sales. It's a specific type of hunger and desire to win that is required to be successful in sales. After high school, I went on to play college football at Austin

Peay State University while majoring in Business with a concentration in Marketing.

I was quiet in class for the most part unless the teacher called on me. The one teacher in college that gave me a hard push in the right direction was Fred Landiss. He was my Salesmanship professor, and our final exam was to create a business and present it to the class. The first thing he said when I completed my presentation was that you have the personality of someone who will make a great salesman. That's all I needed to hear to get me going again. I also worked during college during every school break. Perisian, Fox & Hound, Trane, and Bosch, but the one that pushed me further was Convergys, a call center for AT&T. Here, I gained confidence in talking to people, no matter how mad or frustrated they were.

After graduating, I learned that a marketing career required one to three years of sales experience. Of course, everyone says they want to work in their degree field. After all, earning the degree took 4 to 5 years of hard work and studying. So, the first place I ran to was the hardest and most fast-paced sales you could imagine, CAR SALES. When I say that I got a real crash course in high-pressure sales, that is probably the understatement of the century. Here I was a 22-year old college graduate with no responsibilities other than rent, and I was in here fighting for sales with grown men with families. I failed miserably at the first car lot. I was only there for about a month before they let me go due to attendance. I left that car lot and went down the street to a competitor. I had no idea what I had gotten myself into, but of course, that competitive nature kicked in.

After six months, I had found my groove, and with the help of my trainer, mentor, and now just a close friend, Paul Horton, I had the confidence to sell and close on my own. The lightbulb finally turned on in my head for me. Now, I was making the most money I had ever made at the stage in my life. I stayed at the lot for about two years before leaving to try to advance my career in a management capacity. That didn't last long because that itch for commission-based sales came roaring back. I am now in Retail Small Business Sales. I have received several awards and have been recognized for my efforts. From graduation in 2009 until today, I have been in sales and haven't looked back or had a second thought.

My mother attributes my gift of gab to my father, Glenn Greene, Sr. He was a bartender in his younger days then transitioned into sales as he got older. He has worked in some form of sales for over 20 years. In his years of sales, he has always been among the very best at what he does. He has become my mentor and biggest fan when it comes to sales and how to handle the pressure that comes along with it. We are always sharing stories from the experiences we encounter with our customers. I think I got my compassion and empathy for customers from my mother, Ezma Crawford. She worked in customer service for years and now is a special education teacher. She has the biggest heart of anyone I know.

Introduction

Get to the Greene Sales is not your ordinary book on sales. Most sales books give you all the sunshine and roses of working in sales. I am going to tell you the good, the bad, and the ugly of it. Sales is the most inconsistent industry to be a part of, but that shouldn't discourage you. If it were easy, everyone would do it. What makes you different is the fact that you are even here reading to progress your craft. Notice I didn't say perfect your craft. Sometimes, we focus too much on perfection and don't take time to acknowledge our progress. So, sit back, relax, grab your favorite cigar, or brandy, and let me walk you through the following pages on how to "Get to the Greene."

Chapter 1: Why Sales?

Get paid your worth.

One thing that is an undeniable fact about all people in the working world is that we all want to be paid for the work we do. I can't tell you how many times I have heard people say they feel underpaid or they feel like they are worth so much more to the company. Well, the one thing about working in sales is you are going to get paid for what you do. If you don't sell, you don't get paid; it is as simple as that. Now, of course, some places pay you both base pay and commission, but most of the time, the base pay is minimum wage or something close to it. Very few companies offer you both a healthy base pay as well as a strong commission. In a sense, you usually have to pick your poison. Then, you also have the businesses, like car lots or real estate, where you get paid solely on commission. If "you don't work you don't eat" were a career field, it would definitely be sales. The pay options are easily one of the most significant benefits of working in sales. If I know I want to go on vacation during a certain month and want some extra spending money beyond what I'm already making, I know I simply need to close more deals.

Transferrable Skills

The skills I have learned working in sales work across any industry or walk of life. Believe it or not, we are always selling every single day of our life. You are a walking billboard advertising your life and skills. I always tell people if you can make a friend you can make a sale. There is no difference in asking for a sale and asking someone on a date. So, you've been selling your whole life and didn't even know you were. When you go on a job interview, you are selling the employer on all your features and benefits. The process is just the same as you would with selling a product to a potential customer. When you were a child and wanted to go to that party with your friends, and you needed to convince your parents—you were selling. The same thing happens in life as an adult. When the husband wants to go to the bar with the guys, and he has to get his wife to see things from his point of view, he's selling. I can go on for days with examples of sales in everyday life and how it is used from one walk of life to the next.

Competitive

The most exciting part of working in sales is challenging yourself every hour, every day, every week, and every month to be better than you were before. On top of that, unless you have an exclusive product that is a 1 of 1, you are competing against other salespeople or other competing providers of the same product. The thing that keeps me going each day is trying to outdo whoever is at the top. If I am at the top, then I want to go after whoever has sold at the highest level or has broken some type of record. The object is always to get better and keep striving for greatness. I once read that "greatness is doing small things extraordinarily over and over again." This quote couldn't be truer, so you have to make sure each and every hour of the day you are improving upon the previous hour. Complacency is the biggest threat to greatness.

Ever Changing

Change is inevitable in sales. As the needs and wants of customers change, so does your approach and your product. You have to be willing to evolve and grow with your customer base. Especially in the age of technology with everything going digital, you must be open to change. Millennials have the most substantial buying power in the world right now and seem to be the most indecisive from my experiences. As a millennial myself, I grew up in the age of the internet and grew up with the changes in technology. Keeping up with the rapid pace of changing technology can be challenging. New software or a new device of some sort comes onto the market that connects people to the internet.

Social media changed the landscape of the world. Social media connects people no matter where they are in the world. You have to be willing to change your advertising and marketing strategy to meet your customers where they are. Facebook and

Instagram marketing are at an all-time high, and more businesses are taking to the internet to grow their customer base. In short, it can be summed up in 3 simple words; Evolve or DIE! We will discuss this in greater depth in Chapter 8.

Always something to be sold

When building a good quality relationship with a customer, you should uncover underlying needs that the customer doesn't even know exists. All customers come into your location with one thing in mind. Your job is to introduce them to other products and services you offer. If a customer leaves your store only with what they came for, you are no longer a salesperson—you are a cashier. Your role is no different than a cashier at the grocery store because they only ring out what you bring them. Upselling is an art that takes consistent practice and repetition. Top-down selling is a method that helps you maximize your opportunities no matter how few and far apart they may be. The idea is to start with your higher-end products first that have the most features and benefits and work your way down. This selling strategy is not an attempt to make the customer spend more money; it is to break down the barrier and put additional supplemental items on their mind. Selling with integrity is what earns you a customer versus only making a sale.

Chapter 2: Establish a Goal

Begin with the End in Mind

When working in sales, no two days are ever the same. With that being said, you should start each day knowing what you want to accomplish by the end of the day. Going about the day without thinking it out is going to have you, as they say, "running around like a chicken with your head cut off." In the morning, if you set a goal of scheduling five appointments by the end of the day, you focus your time and efforts on locking down five appointments. Another example, if you go in with the mindset on closing five deals, you focus on closing five deals. The key to a productive day is to plan your work and work your plan.

Identify your target

Have you ever played darts without a board? Exactly! It's impossible to hit the bullseye if there isn't a board or target identified. You have something to strive toward when you have a clearly defined target. You know precisely what you want to accomplish by the end of the month. Whether it is a monetary figure that you are looking for in commissions or a certain amount of sales, always keep this target on your mind. I recommend posting it somewhere so you will see it every day. You should aim for a clear, precise target. Identifying the target is only half the battle. The next step is to determine how you will hit the mark.

Another target you must identify along with your quota is your target market. You must know your potential buyers so you can tailor your approach and technique. You don't want to talk at a high level that is over your customer's head. At the same time, you don't want to speak too vaguely when the customer wants details. You have to know your audience and do what works best for them.

Break your target down into daily wins

Once you have established your target, now you need to break it down into smaller daily wins. Focusing on smaller steps makes the target easier to attain and gets your focus off the big picture. I usually break down my target by dividing the target by the number of workdays in the month. On average, you have 22 working days each month. To keep it simple mathematically, if your target is 220 sales by the end of the month, then you need to close ten sales each day. Life in sales becomes interesting on the days where you over or underachieve. Let's say you have a stellar day and close 13 deals on the first day of the month. Having one fantastic day doesn't mean you only need to close seven the next day. Your target is still ten per day. Your target doesn't change because sales is an inconsistent field, and you have to account for the days you may not hit ten. On the other hand, if you continue to make ten or more sales each day, then you will set yourself apart from your peers. I've never seen a sales manager upset with a rep for overachieving, but they will have a real problem with you underachieving.

How much is your time worth?

I spoke in the previous chapter about being able to make as much money as you desire in sales. That statement carries a lot of weight, but this next question holds just as much weight. How much is your time worth? The average workday is eight hours, right? Using the same example from earlier, if you have broken your target down into ten deals per day, that means you have eight hours to close ten deals. That breaks down to 1.25 sales an hour. Now, of course, you can't close a fourth of a deal, but you can break it down to five deals before lunch. Don't overcomplicate things with math. The acronym K.I.S.S. (Keep It Simple Stupid) can be applied to almost any walk of life, including this. So, after breaking the target down into daily goals, break it down within the hours of the day. Time is the one currency you can never get back once it is spent. Therefore, use it wisely and only on things that will bring you the desired results.

Laser Focus

Now that you have your target clear in your sights, you must stay laser-focused on what you must do to accomplish your goal. In any industry, you encounter distractions, but you must learn to starve your distractions. Don't feed into anything that takes you away from your task. One thing I have always told myself since I first entered the working world is that "I go to work to make money." You leave your home life at home and focus on work while at work. On the flip side, you leave work life at work. I'm not going to sit here and lie to you by saying this is easy because it's not. We are human. We are going to straddle the line at times, but you must know how to separate the two. Turn yourself into a heat-seeking missile only focused on destroying your target.

Chapter 3: Be the Wolf

Be Strategic

The wolf, in my opinion, is the most interesting and cunning animal in the wild. When I tell you to be strategic, I mean that in every sense of the word. Sales is a game for thinkers. You can't go in without a plan. You have to think through every transaction before you even engage the customer. You have to prepare for any and every twist and turn that the sale may take. If you have supplemental products or services to offer, you must know how you will smoothly transition into offering these products and services. A customer can sense when you are rambling, and that can cost you heavily. Be precise in your approach so as not to find yourself making meaningless small talk. We sometimes mistake building rapport with rambling. You can easily get caught up in talking to your customer about hobbies, children, and what they ate last night if you are not careful. Make every conversation and topic that is discussed tie back into the transaction. Even if the customer attempts to steer the conversation, it is your job as the professional to redirect.

Be Patient

A wolf would rather starve than make a mistake. My uncle once told me, "You can't rush good BBQ." This truth can be transferred over to sales as well. You can't rush the sales process. Each step has its own specific purpose in the big scheme of things. If you rush through the process, you will find yourself trying to backtrack, and that only confuses the customer. You want everything to flow as smoothly as possible. To the customer, you are the professional and the face of your company. If you come off as hurried and confused, it makes you and your company appear incompetent. As we all know, bad service travels 20 times faster than good service. So you would have to have 20 good reviews just to make up for that one bad review. Slow down. Take your time. Go through the full process, and you will enjoy that good BBQ.

Know when to attack

After the strategy and patience, you must know when to attack. Sometimes as salespeople, we get too caught up in the process and never do the most important thing. ASK FOR THE SALE. Once you have gone through your spill, dotted all of your I's, and crossed all your T's, it's time to "attack" The customer always gives you cues that they are sold on your product. Words may not always flow from them, but body language is undeniable. If you ever notice the customer nodding their head with you while you are talking, that's a buying signal. Unfolded arms versus folded arms is another tell-tale sign that they are "picking up what you are putting down." The worst thing you can do is talk past the sale.

Beware of the wrong pack

Wolves hang with wolves. Buzzards hang with buzzards. You are a wolf, and you should run with other wolves. The Bible says that iron sharpens iron. If you strive to be the best that you can be in this field, you have no business hanging with buzzards. Wolves strategize and go after their prey. Buzzards live off the scraps that are left behind by the wolves. It's all about the effort you put into your work. The wolf puts forth the necessary effort required to eat and get what they want out of this career. The buzzard doesn't plan, doesn't strategize, or any of the things we've discussed. The buzzard just drifts through the day, waiting for something to fall into their lap.

This is not a circus

Don't allow yourself to get caught up in the horse and pony show sometimes goes on at any workplace. As stated previously, you are here to make money. This piggybacks directly from being a part of the wrong pack. Just like the real circus, the horses and ponies at work travel in packs. You can easily fall by the wayside if you don't have it set in your mind that you will not join the circus. Unless you simply want to be average, then hey, by all means, grab your clown shoes and join the circus. However, if you're going to be great, then you will not allow yourself to fall victim to the big top. Greatness requires effort every single day.

Chapter 4: Embrace Mistakes

Mistakes mean you're trying

One of my favorite quotes is, "If you are not making a lot of mistakes, you are not making enough decisions." If you are genuinely trying your best at anything, not just in sales, you are going to make mistakes. The only way you can avoid failing to close a deal is never to attempt to close one. You have to be willing to stick your neck out there to see what you are missing. In any walk of life, you can't fear failure. Fear of failure is a more significant threat to success than anything else. One thing I adopted quickly in sales was a "Big risk-Big reward" mentality. I would rather aim for the moon and settle for the stars than to aim for the stars and settle for clouds. You can spend your whole day at work on the clock, but if you never try to close a sale, you are wasting your time. Make mistakes. Learn from them. Apply the new-found knowledge.

Fall Forward

As I previously stated, you are going to fall and scuff yourself up, so the same is in business. The object is to fall forward. Fall reaching further out and stretching for new boundaries. Some say it's good to fall on your back because you can still see the top, but I disagree with that. Falling on your back means that you were playing on your heels and not on your toes.

Keep striving for new levels of greatness, and you will always fall forward. My old coach always told us not to get complacent. When you become complacent, that's when you land on your back. Keep striving. Keep grinding.

Progress over perfection

There is no such thing as perfection in this business. That's why I say chase progression, not perfection. Slow and steady progress help you achieve the best version of yourself. You will slowly begin to see things and learn new things about this business with each failure. So, as crazy as it may sound, if you find yourself in a rut, keep going. Who wants to stay in a rut anyway? Exactly! Nobody wants to be in a rut forever. Keep working towards making the most progress that you can with each interaction. Success is a journey, not a destination. Just keep moving forward. The progress you make speaks for itself when you least expect it.

Mistakes are inevitable

Don't get down on yourself for making mistakes. Deion Sanders is arguably the best cornerback ever to play professional football. He has given up touchdowns. He has missed tackles. He has dropped interceptions. You are going to make mistakes in this business. I can't tell you how many times I have misquoted a price to a customer. Countless times, I have accidentally put the wrong address on a package. Mistakes happen. Mistakes mean you are trying as we just learned. As long as the mistakes don't turn into patterns, you are good. Repeating the same mistakes over and over will get you promoted to customer. (You read that right.)

Learn from your mistakes

On the job training is the absolute best training you can get. You then can learn hands-on how to avoid making the same mistakes repeatedly. We now know that mistakes happen and are inevitable. However, failing to learn from mistakes is a choice. The definition of insanity is doing the same thing over and over, expecting a different result. So, if you make the same mistakes repeatedly, you are, well, insane. Companies will only have so much patience with you. Customers, too. Never make a habit of having to apologize for making the same mistakes or doing the same thing that goes against your training. At that point, the manager feels like it's either you are making a mistake intentionally, or you are merely inept.

Chapter 5: Play the Numbers

Law of Averages

One thing about sales is the fact that it is all numbers based. When I say that, I am referencing the fact that everything is based on averages and ratios. When forecasts and quotas are put together, more times than not, computation plays a part. The numbers don't just fall out of the sky. The law of averages was not specifically created for sales, but it is incredibly fitting. It states that if you do something often enough, then a ratio appears. Once the said ratio is established, it continues, and what you lack in skill you make up for in numbers. You don't have to be the greatest salesperson ever to live to be successful. If you are consistent with your message and position yourself into more prospects, you will do well. I once worked with a guy who was not the best salesperson by any stretch of the imagination. He didn't have the best customer service. He didn't have all the product knowledge in the world. He didn't try to come off overly polite with his customer. However, what he did do was work faster and smarter than any of the other reps in the store. THAT is what made him successful in his career.

Lose Fast and Move On

One thing we as salespeople sometimes find ourselves doing is trying to manufacture a sale. When I sold cars, this was a horrible habit of mine. I would get caught up with customers trying to, as they say, "love the one you're with." I would demo the car, go on the test drive, have them in love with the car, and then run the credit. If anyone who is reading this has ever sold cars, you know how backward this process is. This scenario takes anywhere from one to two hours out of my day, but I don't even know if they can afford the vehicle yet. In a perfect world, I would've run credit earlier in the process to establish them as a true buyer first. Doing that, I could either keep going forward with them or politely dismiss them. Lose fast. You want to qualify the customer first before going down the rabbit hole of manufacturing a sale. Especially in the car business because you can easily tie up your day with one customer trying to find a lender. I would say in any business that deals with credit as a way of approvals that should be at the beginning of your sales process. Getting approval first keeps you from wasting your time—and your customer's time as well.

Stay in the fight

Now I know this may sound contradictory following the previous point, but you must stay in the fight. Let me explain this to you before you think I'm just stone crazy. When I say stay in the fight, the other party has to at least be in the fight. Don't stay in the fight with a customer who is unable to buy. We often find ourselves trying to maintain excellent customer service with a customer we have yet to win. You can't overlook the first word, which is CUSTOMER. You have to win the customer before you can start working on customer service. So, first, qualify the customer. Then, once qualified, stay in the fight as long as you can to win their business. As long as the customer is not completely turned off during the process, the fight must go on. Body language is the most significant factor to observe. Body language speaks the truth even when the words don't match.

More Connections = More Sales

It may seem like common sense, but believe me, there are lots of salespeople I have come across that are just not aggressive with gaining more contacts. A friend of mine was once in an interview for an outside sales position. He was asked, "Are you a hunter or a farmer?" This question is so appropriate for the topic and is somewhat similar to the wolf and the buzzard analogy stated earlier. While the hunter goes out looking for kills, the farmer is content with what is easily accessible. Although both require some strategy, the hunter is the aggressor. If I am forming a team of salespeople, I want four hunters over ten farmers any day of the week. Yes, you can touch more customers with more reps; however, I would prefer to have aggressive hunters that I know are hungry versus the complacent farmer. It is similar to how you hear people say they would rather have a few loyal friends over a lot of associates. It is better to have a few great workers than a lot of below-average workers.

More Rounds = Less Aim

The saying, "More Rounds = Less Aim," goes back to the Law of Averages. If you have ever seen someone shoot a machine gun, they can shoot hundreds of rounds and only hit the target twelve times. On the flip side, if you are shooting a revolver, you usually have six chances to hit your target. You must be super accurate and poised to hit with the revolver, whereas with the machine gun, you just have to be in the area. This ties in with sales in the sense that you may not have the best pitch on a product, but the more people you pitch it to, the better your odds. It all boils back down to numbers and averages. Not only do you need to talk to lots of customers, but you also need to be consistent with your approach to close more deals. If you get a talk track that works for you and you use it with every single customer you encounter, you are becoming the machine gun.

Chapter 6: Shoot Your Shot

Worst Thing They Can Say is "No"

One of the biggest fears humans have is rejection. No one likes to hear the word "No." It is just a natural reaction to fear rejection. In sales, that should be the least of your worries. If you are starting at zero and ask to go to step one and you are told no, you are still at zero. You have not lost anything. Rejection is not the end of the world. It just means you have either not sold them on you, the product, or the company you represent. Either way, the battle has only just begun. If you accept the first "No" in sales, you are bound for failure. You may be asking yourself; how do I not accept the first "No," but at the same time, "Lose Fast and Move On?" The difference between the two incidents is simple. Losing fast refers to the customer's ability to buy. Not accepting "No" relates to them being able to buy and just simply giving you a negative response.

You Miss 100% of the Shots you don't take

Imagine watching a basketball game, and neither team is shooting the ball. They are just running up and down the court, turning the ball over left and right. At some point, you must throw the basketball towards the rim, at least. Not shooting the ball avoids mistakes, but it also guarantees that you will never make a shot. The same principle works in a sales environment.

If you never talk to a customer or attempt to close a deal, yes, you won't make any mistakes, but you will also never close any deals. You have to at least make the minimal effort in this business. If you avoid taking chances to close the deal, you will never know where you need to improve.

Not asking the question is accepting "NO" prematurely

This concept reinforces the previous point. Not asking certain questions of the customer is automatically answering the question as "NO." Let's put it in a real-world scenario. Say you are in a relationship with the same person for five years. You all have been living together and have a child. All signs are pointing towards marriage. However, there is one small problem. The man has yet to pop the big question out of fear that she may say no. She is ready for the wedding she has been dreaming about since she was a little girl. He never asks the question. She never gets her dream wedding. All because he accepted "No" without ever asking the question.

What do you have to lose?

I always like to ask sales reps this question when they don't ask customers to purchase additional products. What do you have to lose? You already have the customer's attention. Why wouldn't you ask more questions? Doing so only increases your productivity. If I come to you inquiring about buying a pair of shoes, you are not going to deter me from buying the shoes if you ask me to buy socks too. It is that simple. If a customer wants to buy Item A and you offer them Item B to compliment it, you are not going to lose them for making the offer. In all my years in this business, I have never seen that happen. If you are offering them products that make sense with what they initially came to purchase, you will be just fine. In the unlikely event you lose the whole deal, what have you lost? You never had the sale anyway. Before talking to the customer, you had not sold anything. If, after talking to them, you still haven't sold anything, what have you lost? Hopefully, you lost fast and didn't waste too much of your valuable time.

Trust your shot

Once you shoot your shot, you have to trust yourself. Customers deal with salespeople they like. However, they buy from the salespeople that they trust. If you do not show trust and faith in your abilities, the customer most definitely won't either. When I first started in this business back at the car lot, lacking confidence in myself was my biggest issue. I never had trouble talking to customers and getting them interested in the vehicles. My biggest flaw was when the sales manager gave me the numbers to present to the customer; I got overwhelmed. I was selling with my own pockets in mind. I was fresh out of college and had never considered buying cars priced the way these cars were priced. I would go back to the customer with the sales sheet to go over the numbers thinking in mind, "there is no way they are going to go for this." It took me a few months and a few deals to realize one important thing. They would not be here looking at the vehicles if the price was an issue. Of course, occasionally, you get what they call the "tire kickers," but for the most part, people value their time too much to do that. If you exude enough trust in yourself and your product, the customer has no choice but to follow suit.

Chapter 7: Keep Learning

Education > Entertainment

Education is the one thing that can never be taken away from you. Money comes and goes. Cars get old and depreciate. Shoes and clothes go out of style. The information and knowledge you absorb last forever. I was taught at an early age to educate yourself more than you entertain yourself. When I say entertainment, I do not only mean in the sense of partying and going out. Entertainment can be binge-watching your favorite television show or watching movies all night. Now, do not get me wrong and think everything is all business all the time. We all need a release. You just have to do it in moderation. There is no such thing as knowing everything there is to know. You can never be overeducated in any field. However, you can be below standard in an area. It is much better to have the knowledge and not need it; than to need the knowledge and not have it.

Know the competition

An often-undervalued part of sales is knowing the competition. When you know what the competition has to offer, you have a leg up. For instance, while working at Verizon, we sold pretty much all the same products as our major competitors. One of the differentiating factors between the competitors and us was the promotions we offered at any given time. If I know that my promotion is better than anything they have to offer, that is the equivalent of holding the big joker in spades. No matter what the customer comes with, I know, at the end of the day, I can offer them something that my competition cannot. That is transferrable to any type of sales job you hold. If you know what the others cannot offer, it gives you a competitive advantage. That is why a lot of businesses price match their competitors. That way, even if they do not currently have a promotion or price point to compete, they can match the offer. That is also why most good salespeople will rarely give you an offer in writing. If I provide my customer with a written offer, what's to stop them from taking it to a competitor to have them match the offer?

Product Knowledge

One of the worst things you can tell a customer is that you don't know something about a product that you offer. Customers expect you to be an expert on what you offer. To them, you are the face of the company. You have to replace words and phrases like that from your vocabulary. I don't know. I can't. We don't do that. That's against our policy. All of these should be deleted from your Rolodex of responses to customers. I can find out for you. Let me see what I can do. Let me tell you what I can do. The customer really does not care about your policies. They want you to provide a specific or very similar service for them to meet their needs. If you pay close attention to the replacement phrases, they all offer some type of resolution or at least an attempt. For every problem, there should be some type of solution. It may not always be precisely what the customer wants, but you should be able to offer them something other than an "I don't know."

Practice Objections

Very few customers are going to bite on the first pitch. It is much more likely for them to say no or redirect before saying, "Yes." Knowing that you have to be prepared to address the objections as they come. The only way to prepare is to practice. You practice your rebuttal for your common objections. You will never know how to combat all objections, but you can prepare for the ones you hear most frequently. Preparation helps you become more confident when objections and complaints arise. You will never have the answer to every single objection, but you can learn to be the best at overcoming them. Practice makes progress. Perfection doesn't exist, so don't beat yourself up, trying to accomplish an impossible feat. The goal is to improve daily.

READ! READ! READ!

You may think telling you to read is a moot point considering you are reading this book. However, merely picking up a book and reading is the best way to educate yourself on your craft. I know in this age of vast technology with e-books and audiobooks readily available, many people don't buy hard copies. I find it much easier and more gratifying to be able to put my hands on a book physically. Seeing the words on the page and actually being able to feel the pages turn in your hands is a different vibe. The information is the same either way, but it can be received differently based on the delivery. No matter what delivery method you choose, I recommend that you read as much as you can, as often as you can. A lot of the knowledge I have gained over the years came from books I've read. My personal favorite authors are Robert Greene, Grant Cardone, and Zig Ziglar. Cardone and Ziglar are known as two of the hands-down best salesmen ever to live. Robert Greene focuses on your mindset and how you approach life. If you are going to do any considerable amount of reading, I would put them at the top of my list and, of course, myself, Justin Greene.

Chapter 8: Be Open to Change

Evolve or DIE!

We are in an ever-changing environment. The world is changing more and more every single day. Just think about the last 20 years how much has changed. Calls have become text messages. Writing letters has turned into sending emails. Applying for a job all takes place online. Long-distance calls have been replaced by looking someone up on social media. What makes you think that the sales industry would stay the same? Customers are no longer interested in spending their whole day at a car lot waiting on financing and test driving cars. Everything is at a fast-food pace. Instant gratification is more rampant than ever before. We, as sales professionals, must evolve with the times. You have to do whatever it takes to put yourself in front of as many prospects as possible. If you are not talking to a potential buyer every working day, then you are cheating yourself. In the time I have been in the business, I have seen things change dramatically when it comes to getting customers' attention. However, the one thing that has stayed the same is the fact that things are bound to change.

Millennial Movement

Millennials hold by far the most substantial buying power. Projections show that this group alone spends just over

$1 trillion annually. That's trillion with a "T." It would behoove you to focus your marketing strategies around the interests of the group with the largest buying power. I'm not saying to ignore the other groups by any means. What I am saying is to focus your efforts on who has the potential to spend the most money with you. You have to be willing to adjust your strategy to fit your audience. It's all about meeting the customer where they are. When I sold cars we were taught, when the sales manager comes in the office to close your deal, you get down to eye level or lower on the same side of the table as the customer. You have to bend and move with what works for each client. Millennials are heavy into text messaging and the virtual age.

Tech Wave

Technology is all around us. When phones pretty much became small computers, that was as big of a sign as flashing red lights before a cliff that times were changing! The world as we knew it would never be the same. Everything is now online. No one even goes to the library anymore. Dictionaries are a thing of the past. Everything you want or need is in your pocket at the touch of a finger. You have to adjust and redirect to fit the times. If your target market is all younger generation buyers, millennials and younger, then you shouldn't have many paper ads. You should focus your efforts on social media marketing and email blasts. On the flip side, if you are catering to an older audience, they may appreciate that flyer in the mail or a phone call. It's all about the customer.

Old habits still work

Now I know this may sound contradictory to the previous points, but sometimes you have to stick to the old tricks. As much as people like to do everything digitally, nothing is more effective than meeting a customer face to face. I worked in small business sales for over five years. Most customers would say call or email them. They would read the emails and fail to respond, or whenever I called, they would be "busy." Once I decided that I was tired of getting the runaround and went directly to their business, I saw a change in my results. In a face to face encounter, you understand body language and facial expressions. These are the things you can't pick up over the phone. Customers love to feel special. When they see you put forth the effort to come to their establishment, it will set you aside from the competition. Everyone is going to call them and try to get past the illustrious gatekeeper. Not many are going to get in their car and pull up. When in doubt and the customer seems to be hard to reach by phone, go to them.

Grow with your clientele

As you continue to grow in your business, your clientele will increase. The longer you stay in business, you will begin to see repeat customers and referrals. You have to be able to grow with your clientele. When I say that I mean as their needs change, you have to be there and address them. Just like anything else, customers grow and change. I had a customer that owned a small family-owned flower shop—nothing major, just a local florist delivering arrangements to nearby customers on holidays and funerals. Once again, the business was nothing over the top or heavyweight. As time went on, the company began to grow. What started as a single location turned into multiple locations. Of course, as they grew, their needs changed over time. They no longer just needed a few phones for the family members. Now, the business required phones, tablets, office phones, and vehicle tracking. This type of growth is what you love to see. Another example involves a customer who grew in their abilities. Maybe that customer you have always had that didn't want to give up old habits now prefers an email over a call. Subtle changes are still changes nonetheless. You, as the sales professional, must be flexible and make it happen either way.

Chapter 9: Close it Down

Ask for the sale

Some of the things you think should be so easy sometimes are often challenging to do. Many sales professionals go through the entire process but miss the main part. Once you have done all that you can do, the final step is to ask for the sale. One reason this step is often overlooked is that we get lost in building rapport, and the customer ends up guiding the sale. At all times, you must control the narrative of the deal. Once you lose control, it is hard—but not impossible—to get it back. Asking for the sale can come in many different forms. In the car business, they say after presenting your numbers, you extend the pen and remain silent. Whoever breaks the silence first loses. My personal favorite closing question is, "Fair enough?" That phrase removes some of the sting out of making the purchase. "Mr. Customer, here are the terms that you requested. If, in any event, you should decide you are unhappy, you have 30 days to return your device—no harm, no foul. Fair enough?" That's just one example of how to use it. As you notice, I also included the return policy, which can differ from one company to the next. Full disclosure in this business is paramount. You never want to be looked at as the grimy salesman. Sales is by far the most rewarding business to be in, but also it is the most criticized. When asking for the sale, be sure to disclose all pertinent information, so the customer is made aware of all options. It is better to make a customer than to make a sale.

Keep the Yes's coming

Once you get the customer saying yes to your questions, it is your job to keep them on that track. You can help with this by subtly nodding your head in approval while asking your questions. More times than not, the customer will unconsciously agree with you just from your body language. Now let's be clear, I'm not saying to hoodwink the customer into doing business with you. It is your job to make sure they know the terms of the agreement. Whether the question is big or small, once you get to the point that things are agreeable, it becomes a pattern. You sometimes have to get creative to keep it going, but it is beneficial. With being creative, you still need to remember the end goal. Don't ask questions that lead you down a rabbit hole of irrelevancy. The worst thing you can do is get caught up talking to the customer about the price of tea in China. Your time is too valuable to get lost in meaningless small talk. You don't have to be cookie-cutter decisive at all times of the transaction. You also don't want to be the salesman who spends more time making friends with the customer instead of making money.

Don't Over Sell

In the process of selling, we sometimes find ourselves overselling. This practice is not uncommon, but I'm here to tell you it is counterproductive. It usually happens when the customer has gone silent while thinking. We frequently equate their silence to reluctance, when in actuality, they are just processing the information. Just put yourself in the customer's shoes temporarily. You just spent around 30 to 45 minutes explaining to them why your product is better than what the competitor offers. The amount of information can be overwhelming to the customer, especially if they came in undecided from the beginning. You have to allow the customer some time to think about the purchase they are about to make. Sometimes, I so step away from the customer for a few moments. Then, they have a few minutes to think and allows me time to prepare for any last-minute objections. It is far better to take time and gather your thoughts than to be stomped by a question you didn't see coming. Besides, as I stated, you just spent nearly an hour with this customer. I'm sure you would like to get the prize at the end.

Confidence is Key

The fact that "Confidence is key" cannot be stated enough. This thought goes hand in hand with what we discussed in Chapter 6 about trusting your shot. You have to exude a level of confidence so high that the customer believes you are the expert in your field. You want the customer to feel that you're not just an expert with your product but with your entire field. If you work for Firestone, after speaking with you, they should believe you are the tire guru. If you work for Chevrolet, you need to be viewed as the go-to man for all things pertaining to cars. When the customer has trust in your product knowledge, they will then trust you with their business. An old but true saying learned early in business goes like this, "Customers talk to who they like, but they buy from who they trust." If you are not speaking with confidence and knowledge about your product, it's highly unlikely that they will buy from you. Confidence starts with your body language and follows through with the words you speak. Eye contact is critical. Stand up or sit up straight while talking to the customer. Finally, speak clearly and assertively. If you are stumbling over your words, it will come off as you are unsure. Increase your confidence and increase your sales.

Tell a Friend

We've all heard the old cliché, "Good news travels fast." In sales, you want your customers to sing your praises to all their friends and family. Referrals are the best customers to have for many reasons. To begin with, they have already heard great things about you; otherwise, they wouldn't be contacting you. When you encounter a referral customer, they have already heard great things about you from a trusted source. The best way to influence your customers to refer you more business is to offer them an incentive. In the car business, they call it a bird dog fee. Some places simply call it a referral program. It may come in the form of a discount, gift card, or cash. Also, they are usually effortless to close. The times I've had customers referred to me, there was not much negotiating needed. As I stated, you already have their trust, so they usually offer little resistance. Finally, they will often refer you to even more business. Once you have taken care of them well, they will gladly refer you to their friends and family. Referrals make your job much easier because you will have a seemingly never-ending flow of customers coming in asking for you. The one thing you must remember to do to get a referral is to ask for it. At the end of each sale, you must make it a habit to ask the customer for referrals. "Mr. Customer, if I've taken good care of you and you know of anyone else that could benefit from my products or services, feel free to give them my contact information." Always give your customers several of your business cards. And don't be afraid to follow up with them on it. You were planning to call them back for a general satisfaction follow up anyway, so just add that to the call. "Hey, Mr. Customer just wanted to make sure you were still happy with what I sold. Ok, great also was touching base to see if you know anyone who may need my products or services." They will appreciate the call because most salespeople fail to follow up. Hearing from you will show them that they are more to you than just another sale.

Final Thought

As you can see, the art of selling has many parts. You have to navigate through this maze as seamlessly as possible to have the most success. Don't get me wrong. Depending on who you talk with, these steps will vary. However, the end goal is always the same. The sole reason you get into the sales business is to make money. There is no other reason. You may get different politically correct answers from people depending on the setting in which you ask the question. At the end of the day, we are all here to make money. Once we get a taste of the sales bug, the hardest thing to do is to turn away from it. It almost turns into a high, and we are fiending for our fix. My way may not be the right way, but it's my way—it's what works for me. I hope after reading this book, you achieve all the success you aspire to in this business. Always remember to...

GET TO THE GREENE!

www.ingramcontent.com/pod-product-compliance
Lightning Source LLC
Chambersburg PA
CBHW030537220526
45463CB00007B/2876